How to Draw the Life and Times of
James Monroe

Miriam J. Gross

The Rosen Publishing Group's
PowerKids Press™
New York

For my parents and my brother

Published in 2006 by The Rosen Publishing Group, Inc.
29 East 21st Street, New York, NY 10010

First Edition

Editor: Daryl Heller
Book Design: Julio A. Gil

Illustrations: All illustrations by Holly Ceffrey
Photo Credits: pp. 4, 7, 18, 20, 28 © Bettmann/Corbis; p. 8 © Lee Snider/Photo Images/Corbis; p. 9 Picture History; p. 10 © North Wind Picture Archives; pp. 12, 14 Courtesy of the James Monroe Museum and Memorial Library, Fredericksberg, Virginia; p. 16 © Robert Holmes/Corbis; p. 22 National Museum of American History, Smithsonian Institution, Division of Social History, Textiles; p. 24 One Mile Up; p. 26 (top) © Darrell Gulin/Corbis; p. 26 (bottom) HABS Photo:Jack E. Boucher

Library of Congress Cataloging-in-Publication Data

Gross, Miriam J.
How to draw the life and times of James Monroe / Miriam J. Gross.
      p. cm. — (A kid's guide to drawing the presidents of the United States of America)
Includes bibliographical references and index.
ISBN 1-4042-2982-5 (lib. bdg.)
1. Monroe, James, 1758–1831—Juvenile literature. 2. Presidents—United States—Biography—Juvenile literature. 3. Drawing—Technique—Juvenile literature. I. Title. II. Series.
E372.G76 2006
973.5'4'092—dc22

                                                    2004014517

Manufactured in the United States of America

Contents

Early History

As a young man, James Monroe took part in the American colonies' struggle for independence from Britain. He was the last president to have fought in the American Revolution. Monroe spent his life trying to strengthen the nation whose independence he helped win.

Monroe was born on April 28, 1758, in Westmoreland County, Virginia. His father, Spence Monroe, owned a modest plantation. Monroe spent his childhood roaming the land, riding horses, and hunting. He began his education at the Campbelltown Academy, where he did best in Latin and math. Monroe's father died when the boy was 16. His uncle Joseph Jones became a role model for James. Jones encouraged Monroe to study at the College of William and Mary in Williamsburg, Virginia.

Monroe left college two years later, in 1776, to join the army during the American Revolution. After several years in the military, he returned to

Williamsburg and studied law. In 1782, Monroe won a seat in the Virginia House of Delegates, which made laws for the state. Monroe went on to serve in an early form of the U.S. government called the Congress of the Confederation from 1783 to 1786. In Congress he worked to strengthen the power of the federal government. Virginians elected Monroe to the U.S. Senate in 1790.

Monroe was later appointed as a U.S. diplomat to Europe. Beginning in 1799, he also served three terms as governor of Virginia. In 1811, he accepted an appointment as President James Madison's secretary of state.

You will need the following supplies to draw the life and times of James Monroe:

✓ A sketch pad   ✓ An eraser   ✓ A pencil   ✓ A ruler

These are some of the shapes and drawing terms you need to know:

Horizontal Line	——	Squiggly Line	⟿
Oval	⬭	Trapezoid	⬡
Rectangle	▭	Triangle	△
Shading	▬	Vertical Line	|
Slanted Line	/	Wavy Line	⌇

The Presidency

James Monroe became the U.S. president in 1817. His cabinet, or people who advised him, included Secretary of State John Q. Adams, Secretary of the Treasury William H. Crawford, Secretary of War John C. Calhoun, and Attorney General William Wirt.

Monroe ran successfully for a second term of office in 1820. Throughout both terms, he worked to convince the countries of Europe that the United States was an independent nation and the most powerful force in North America and South America. In December 1823, Monroe gave his annual address to Congress. He stated that the Americas were closed to further European colonization. The United States would not interfere with any existing European colony in the Americas or in any conflict in Europe. However, it would not allow any foreign armed forces in the Western Hemisphere, or the western half of Earth that contains North America and South America. This warning later became known as the Monroe Doctrine.

James Monroe consulted his six cabinet members before making any important decisions. Each cabinet member directs a department of the executive branch of the federal government.

James Monroe's Virginia

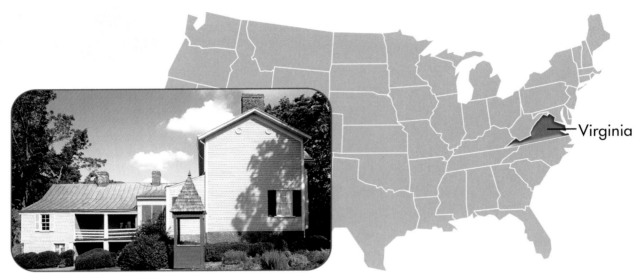

This farmhouse is part of Ash Lawn-Highland, an estate where James Monroe once lived.

Map of the United States of America

Virginia

James Monroe's relatives had first made their home in Westmoreland County, Virginia, near the Potomac River. This county was also where U.S. president George Washington was born. Monroe's birthplace in Westmoreland County has become a monument and a park.

In 1793, James Monroe built a small farmhouse on a 3,500-acre (1,416 ha) plantation next to Thomas Jefferson's estate, Monticello. Monroe named the estate Highland and made it his official home until 1823. The estate was renamed Ash Lawn-Highland after Monroe's death. The College of William and Mary now owns the property, which contains a working farm, a performing arts center, a statue of James Monroe, and belongings of the Monroe family. These belongings include the Monroes' furniture and china, and newspapers from the time of Monroe's presidency. The Ash Lawn-Highland estate is open to the public.

James Monroe was originally buried in New York in 1831. The people of Virginia thought Monroe should be buried in Virginia. Monroe's remains were reburied in 1858 in a magnificent grave at the Hollywood Cemetery in Richmond, Virginia.

Monroe's tomb in Hollywood Cemetery is made of cast iron. To make objects from cast iron, hot iron is poured into a hollow form. Once the metal cools, it hardens into the shape of the form, which is often decorative.

Monroe and the American Revolution

In 1776, when James Monroe turned 18, the American Revolution erupted. The American colonies were angry over taxes and other limits the British government had

imposed on them. Demanding independence, the colonists refused to pay taxes without having a voice in how they were to be governed. Monroe joined a militia known as the Third Virginia Regiment. Monroe's troop marched to New York, where they joined General George Washington's Continental army.

In December 1776, Monroe took part in the famous crossing of the Delaware River to fight British troops in Trenton, New Jersey. The Americans won the battle, and Monroe was advanced to captain for his bravery. In June 1778, he fought in the Battle of Monmouth in New Jersey, which is pictured above.

On October 19, 1781, American troops defeated the British in the Battle of Yorktown. This victory, made possible by the help of the French army and naval forces, ended the war.

1

To begin drawing this scene from the Battle of Monmouth draw the guidelines, as shown. Add an oval and nine straight lines. These lines will be erased later.

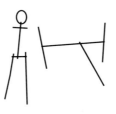

2

Draw the outline of the soldier's body. You will add clothes later. Draw the circle and the line on the cannon guidelines, as shown.

3

Erase the straight body guidelines. Draw the back of the soldier's jacket. Add the face. Draw large ovals for the wheels. Add straight lines to the left wheel and a curved line to the right wheel.

4

Erase extra lines. Finish adding the clothing, including a hat, pants, and boots. Add an arm. Add a line to the wheel on the left. Draw shapes coming from both wheels, as shown.

5

Erase the head oval. Draw the hair. Erase the rough body outlines. Draw details and wrinkles on the clothing. Draw the legs of the cannon. Add an oval to the right wheel, as shown.

6

Draw a bag on the soldier. Draw a long sword in the soldier's hand. Erase the guidelines of the cannon. Add spokes to the wheels.

7

Draw the cannon. Draw details on the legs of the cannon. The Battle of Monmouth was a long battle fought on a hot summer day. Neither side clearly won the battle.

8

Erase the remaining guidelines. Finish with detailed shading. The hat, boots, and jacket are dark. Some of the spokes on the cannon are dark, too.

Elizabeth Kortright Monroe

Elizabeth Kortright met James Monroe when he was a delegate to the Continental Congress in New York. The two were married in 1786. They enjoyed a happy marriage and were rarely apart. The couple had three children. One child died young, however.

After her husband was elected president in 1816, Elizabeth Monroe organized public gatherings that were held in the White House. A private person, she did not like the social obligations, or duties, expected of the wife of a president. The public delighted in the First Lady's taste in clothes and furniture. They were unhappy, however, that she would not make social calls to visit Washington's citizens in their homes.

Elizabeth Monroe's health failed during Monroe's second term. She was often away from Washington, either at the family's Virginia estate, or visiting her daughter Maria in New York. The First Lady let her daughter Eliza lead formal events at the White House. Elizabeth Monroe died on September 23, 1830.

1

Begin by drawing an oval for the head of Elizabeth Kortright Monroe. This will be erased later. Draw a line for the length of the neck and the upper body.

2

Add a slanting oval for the ear. Draw guidelines for the eyes, nose, and mouth. Draw lines for the shoulders and the arms.

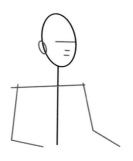

3

Erase the part of the head oval that goes through the ear oval. Draw almond-shaped ovals for the eyes. Draw Elizabeth's jaw and cheek. Draw an outline for the neck, shoulders, and arms.

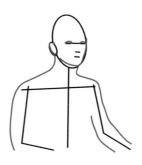

4

Erase the lower part of the head oval. Erase the eye guideline. Draw eyebrows, a nose, and a mouth. Draw circles in the eyes. Draw her cap. Begin to draw the clothing.

5

Erase extra lines in the head and the body. Draw eyelids and pupils. Erase parts of the circles that go through the eyelids. Draw her earring, hair, and lines in her ear. Draw the rest of her clothing. Add the dots to the band of her cap.

6

Erase any remaining body lines that go through the clothing. Finish with detailed shading. The top of her head and her dress are very dark. Her skin is light. You can shade the background by using the side of your pencil tip. You can blend your pencil lines by using your finger or a Q-tip.

Monroe as U.S. Minister to France

In 1789, the people of France overthrew their monarchy during the French Revolution. Britain and other European monarchies feared that the revolution would spread across Europe, and they sought to stop it. American politicians were divided over the French Revolution.

In 1794, President Washington appointed James Monroe U.S. minister to France. Monroe's task was to assure the French that the United States would remain neutral in France's conflict with Britain. Unfortunately, Secretary of State Edmund Randolph did not tell Monroe that John Jay had been sent to negotiate a U.S. treaty with Britain. Monroe was furious when he learned of the treaty. He felt that the United States owed a debt to France for their aid during the American Revolution. President Washington recalled Monroe from France in 1796.

Monroe bought the desk shown above in Europe. Among the documents Monroe wrote at this desk was the speech later known as the Monroe Doctrine.

1

James Monroe purchased the desk that is shown at left in Europe, when he was the U.S. minister to France. To begin drawing the desk, use a ruler to draw a trapezoid.

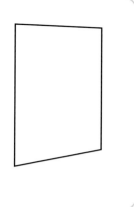

2

Add a leg to the lower left corner. Add three lines to the left side. These lines add depth, or thickness, to the desk.

3

Add the other three legs. Draw two vertical lines and one horizontal line on the front. Add a slightly sloping line on the left side.

4

Add a line above the line you just drew. Erase the lines that go through the legs. Draw the writing surface. It is a shape with slanted sides. Connect it to the horizontal line using a vertical line.

5

Erase the lines of the desk that go through the writing surface. Add an edge to the board, as shown. Add trim lines to the top of the desk. Draw the lines inside the desk.

6

Draw a drawer near the top. Add two squiggly lines for the handles. Draw the lines near the bottom. Add shelves inside.

7

Add thick lines near the sides. Draw horizontal lines to make drawers. Add circles for the handles. Draw more detail lines near the bottom.

8

Finish with shading. Notice the areas that are the darkest. Monroe's desk had two secret compartments, or places, which Monroe used to store special letters.

The Louisiana Purchase

In 1803, President Thomas Jefferson sent James Monroe back to Paris to help Robert R. Livingston, the U.S. minister to France, negotiate a land purchase from France. The

French had settled the territory between the Mississippi River and the Rocky Mountains and had named it Louisiana after King Louis XIV. In 1762, France gave the territory to Spain. The United States signed a treaty with Spain in 1795 that gave the United States the right to sail on the Mississippi and to ship goods from the port city of New Orleans.

When Spain returned Louisiana to France in 1801, the United States worried that it would lose these rights. Jefferson sent Livingston and Monroe to purchase only New Orleans and part of Florida to protect these rights. However, when the French emperor Napoléon Bonaparte offered to sell the entire Louisiana Territory, the two American ministers gladly accepted. The 1803 Louisiana Purchase was signed in the Cabildo, shown above, which is located in New Orleans.

1

The Louisiana Purchase included land that later became a number of U.S. states. The agreement was signed in the Cabildo. Use a ruler to draw the basic shape of the Cabildo.

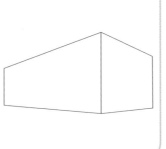

2

Draw the lines on the building, as shown. Some are vertical lines and some are slanted. Connect the lines along the top and in the middle of the building using short slanted lines.

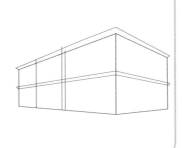

3

Add another edge to the top of your building, as shown. Draw the roof. Add two upside-down V's in the roof area. Draw arched doorways and two windows.

4

Draw more arches. Draw the sides to the arching doorways you drew in step 3. Draw the first window for the roof, as shown. Begin to draw the center tower.

5

Erase extra lines. Add shapes to tower. Draw 11 more roof windows. Add vertical lines to the center section of the building. Add sides to arches. Draw two more rectangular windows.

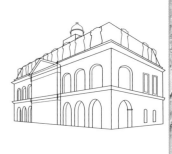

6

Erase extra lines. Add windows and a spike to the top of the tower. Add lines to the tower's base. Add lines to roof windows and to the building. Draw four columns and arches.

7

Draw railings on the second-floor windows. Add backs to roof windows on the right. Add lines to bottom row of arches for columns. Add more arches, lines, and flags to the building.

8

Erase the lines of the building that go through the flags and column bases. Add more details to the windows and roof. Shade the drawing.

The War of 1812

From about 1793 until 1815, Britain and France were at war. The United States tried to stay neutral in the conflict, but Britain refused to respect U.S. neutrality. The British attacked American ships and captured American sailors whom they falsely accused of being deserters from the British navy. On June 1, 1812, President James Madison asked Congress to declare war on Britain. James Monroe, who was then secretary of state, warned Secretary of War John Armstrong that the British might attack the U.S. capital. Armstrong did not listen. In August 1814, British forces captured Washington, D.C. Armstrong quit. Monroe became secretary of war while still serving as secretary of state.

Monroe made sure that American troops were well armed. He also wrote to General Andrew Jackson and urged him to go to New Orleans to fight the British. On January 8, 1815, Jackson led a group of American forces to a proud victory in New Orleans.

1

To draw Andrew Jackson and his horse at the Battle of New Orleans, first draw two large circles. The left circle is slightly larger than the right. Join the circles with a line.

2

Add lines for three of the horse's legs. You will erase these later. Draw two circles and additional lines for the head and neck, as shown.

3

Draw the outline of the horse. Use your guidelines to help you judge the shape of the sloping neck and back. Draw the shape of the legs carefully, too.

4

Erase the horse guidelines. Leave the head circles until later. Add eyes, ears, a mane, and a tail. Add lines to make hooves and to show muscles in the legs. Draw a stick figure man.

5

Draw the outline of the man. Add a hat and an eye. Erase the large head circle on the horse. Add a circle and another line to the nose circle on the horse.

6

Erase the guidelines for the man. Add hair and clothing. Erase the nose circle on the horse. Add a blanket and a saddle. Add a Y to the horse's chest. Add the final leg of the horse.

7

Erase extra lines. Add stirrups and a sword. Add the shapes and lines to the front of the saddle. Draw a bridle and rope around the horse's head. Add the front of the mane.

8

Erase the lines inside the sword. Finish with shading. The boots and jacket are dark, as are the horse's eyes, mane, tail, and left hind leg. Shade the ground beneath the horse's hooves.

President Monroe Tours the Union

On March 4, 1817, James Monroe was sworn in as the fifth president of the United States. One challenge facing the new president was the growing divisions between

different parts of the country. The South was largely composed of farms and forests. Southerners depended on slaves to farm their plantations. The North was more focused on business. Northerners produced goods on machines in factories. President Monroe wanted the different regions and political groups to work together in spite of these differences.

In order to work toward this goal and gain support for his government, Monroe began his presidency with a long tour across the country. Starting in Maryland, he traveled through Pennsylvania and New York, into New England, and as far west as Detroit. On this trip Monroe became the first U.S. president to travel in a steamboat, which was just becoming popular after its invention by Robert Fulton in 1807.

1

To begin drawing the *Clermont*, a steamboat created by Robert Fulton, draw the boat body in the water. The line for the water is squiggly.

2

Draw the pole and the circles. There are three circles, two of the circles are inside the larger circle. Draw the small cabin. It is like a small rectangular box, but the bottom cannot be seen.

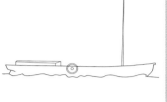

3

Add another pole. Draw a slanted line on the first pole. Add the large smokestack. It has an oval at the top. Draw windows on the cabin. Add lines to the circle. These will become paddles.

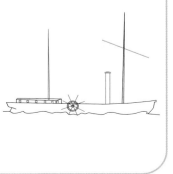

4

Add a slanted line to the left pole. Add the flags and ropes, as shown. Draw a folded-up sail on the first pole. Draw the two shapes next to the smokestack, as shown.

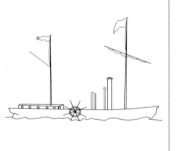

5

Add small vertical lines to the shape just to the left of the smokestack. Draw the large sail. Add the ropes to the pole on the right. Draw the rail at the back of the cabin. Add lines to the paddles.

6

Add the rail to the front of the boat. Add a curved line to the paddles. Add ropes to the boat. To add the tent above the paddles, draw the ropes that hold it up. Then draw the tent.

7

Draw peaks where the ropes touch the tent. Add ropes. Draw smoke. Add lines to the paddles and water under them. Write "Clermont" on the boat.

8

Erase the lines of the tent beneath the peaks. Erase extra lines in the paddles. Add a shape to the corner of the flag on the right. Finish with shading.

The Missouri Compromise of 1820

One issue that President Monroe faced was slavery. Many northerners believed that slavery had to end. Most southern states held that only the states could decide whether to allow slavery within their borders. The 1793  invention of the cotton gin had made harvesting cotton easier. Southerners used many slaves to grow this profitable crop. In 1819, the Missouri Territory, which was part of the Louisiana Purchase, applied to enter the Union as a slave state. Northerners wanted to admit Missouri only if it banned slavery. Southerners thought the federal government had no right to set such limits. Monroe believed that slavery was bad for the country, but he also supported the rights of states to make their own laws. Monroe and his government reached a short-term answer with the 1820 Missouri Compromise. Missouri was admitted to the Union as a slave state, and Maine was admitted as a free state. Slavery was banned in the rest of the Louisiana Purchase territory north of Missouri's southern border.

1

To draw a cotton gin, use your ruler to draw a rectangle. This will be a guide. The sides will be erased later. Draw the handle on the top of the rectangle. Draw the angle on the left side.

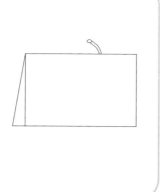

2

Erase the left side of the rectangle. Finish the handle using curved shapes. Draw a shape on the bottom of the rectangle. Draw lines for the right side. Notice how the top right line is drawn.

3

Add the edges to the cotton gin, as shown, using vertical and horizontal lines. Draw ovals on the side of the cotton gin. There is one larger oval and three smaller ones. These are wheels.

4

Erase the right side of the rectangle and the top right corner. Draw lines down the center. Add squiggly edges to the right side. Add ovals inside the large wheel. Draw a ribbon to connect the wheels.

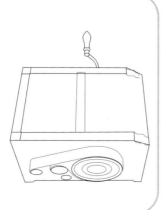

5

Draw more of the ribbon. Add more ovals to the wheels. Draw the shapes inside the gin. There will be several more. Study where they go. One of the shapes is the right edge.

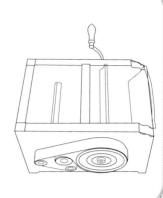

6

Erase extra lines. Add shapes and curvy lines as shown. Add bristles, or combing hairs, to the long shape on the left. Add more ovals and other shapes to the side of the gin.

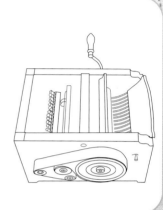

7

Finish the shapes in the gin, as shown. Draw squiggly lines for the cotton on the right side. There are more bristles and more curvy lines. Add lines to the wheel side of the gin.

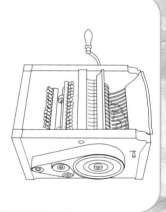

8

Erase the lines of the center shapes that run through the bristles. Finish with shading. Some parts of the gin are dark, others are light. The bristles cast a shadow on the left side of the gin.

Liberia and Monrovia

In 1816, a white New Jersey minister named Robert Finley established the American Colonization Society (ACS). Finley believed that African Americans would never be treated as equals in the United

States. He hoped to start a colony in Africa where freed slaves could live in peace. In 1821, the ACS acquired a piece of land on the western coast of Africa and called it Liberia.

James Monroe supported the ACS and an earlier 1808 congressional ban on the shipment of slaves to the United States. Hoping to end the international slave trade, Monroe helped pass an 1819 bill that funded the return of illegally captured Africans to Africa. He later allowed federal funds to be used in support of Liberia. To thank President Monroe, the ACS named the Liberian capital Monrovia. Liberia became an independent nation in 1847. By 1865, more than 10,000 African Americans had settled there.

1 The seal on the opposite page is the official symbol of Liberia. To begin creating the seal draw a large oval. Add curving lines that meet at points to the top and bottom of the oval.

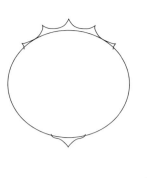

2 Erase the part of the oval that overlaps the shapes you drew in step 1. Add more shapes and lines to the top and bottom of the oval as shown. Draw a horizontal line across the center of the oval.

3 Erase extra lines. Begin drawing the banners above and below the seal. Draw the curved lines on each side of the seal. Add more shapes to the bottom of the seal. Add a ship inside the seal.

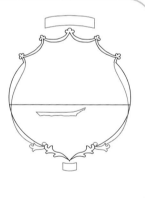

4 Erase the guides. Add shapes to the seal's sides. Continue to draw the banners. Write "LIBERTY" on the top banner and "OF" on the bottom one. Add poles to the ship. Begin the tree, the bird, and the shovel.

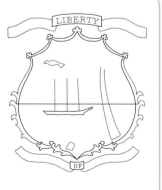

5 Add shapes to the top and the bottom of the banner as shown. Write "THE LOVE OF" and "BROUGHT YOU HERE" in the top banner. Add wings to the bird, lines to the tree trunk, a boat sail, and the sun. Draw a circle to start the plow.

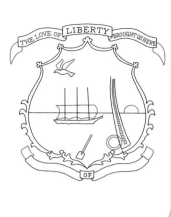

6 Erase extra lines. Add shapes and words to the bottom banner. Write "REPUBLIC" and "LIBERIA." Draw the paper that hangs from the bird's beak. Add leaves and lines to the tree. Add more sails. Draw more of the plow. Add sun's rays.

7 Erase extra lines. Add shapes and lines to the banners. Add details to the tree and the sun. Draw the plow handles and wheel spokes. Add sails. Draw a squiggle for the water.

8 Erase any lines that overlap any new shapes. Finish by shading. The sky, the tree trunk, and the ground are darker than the other areas of the drawing.

Monroe's Retirement

James Monroe was glad to leave office when his second presidential term ended in 1825. He retired to his Virginia estate, Oak Hill, shown here. The estate was named for the many oaks that Monroe planted on the property. Monroe joined the Board of Visitors of the University of Virginia and participated in Virginia's 1829 Constitutional Convention. Monroe began work on his autobiography in 1829. Sadly, the low pay for his public service and the money he had lent his country during his presidency had put Monroe deep in debt. He spent much of his retirement appealing to Congress to pay him back for his expenses. In 1831, Congress granted him $30,000.

The death of his wife, Elizabeth, in 1830 had been a terrible loss for Monroe. His own health was also poor. His daughters believed that he was too weak and lonely to look after himself at Oak Hill. Monroe went to stay with his daughter Maria and her husband in New York City for the last 10 months of his life.

1

At Oak Hill James Monroe planted one oak tree for each state in the Union. To begin drawing an oak tree, draw the trunk and the grass using squiggly lines.

2

Add squiggly lines to the tree for limbs. They don't have to be perfect. Many of the limbs will be covered with leaves. Erase the line for the grass that runs through the trunk.

3

Add more limbs to the tree. Notice how the branches cross each other. Draw the ground beneath the trunk. The line is bumpy and slopes to the right. Oak trees are considered shade trees because they offer good shelter from the sun.

4

Add even more limbs. You should have the general shape of the tree now. The fruit that grows on an older oak tree is the acorn. Squirrels eat acorns when they drop from oak trees in the fall.

5

Draw a bunch of squiggly shapes for leaves. The leaves are in clusters. The top of the tree has a big squiggly shape, and the bottom of the tree has a bunch of smaller shapes or clusters.

6

Erase the lines of the limbs that run through the leaf shapes. Use the side of your pencil to shade in the leaves. Draw squiggly lines all over. Some lines are dark, others are light. Shade the edges of the trunk dark. Draw squiggly lines for grass. Shade to create a shadow under the tree.

Death and Legacy

James Monroe died in New York City at age 73 on the Fourth of July, 1831. New York City hosted a grand funeral for him. Cities throughout the United States observed a day of mourning in his honor. President Andrew Jackson ordered a 24-gun salute, and newspapers recalled Monroe's heroism in the American Revolution and his part in the Louisiana Purchase.

President Monroe helped shape the image of the United States. With the Monroe Doctrine, he made the world view the United States as a strong and independent power. This doctrine continued to affect U.S. foreign policy, or guidelines, well into the twentieth century. President John F. Kennedy used the Monroe Doctrine in 1962 to oppose Soviet activity in Cuba. James Monroe helped extend the boundaries of the young nation across the continent, and he worked to make the American people see themselves as part of one nation.

1

To draw James Monroe, begin by drawing the head oval. This will be erased later. Draw a line for Monroe's neck and upper body.

2

Add horizontal guidelines for the eyes, nose, and lips. Draw a curve for the side of the head next to the head oval. Draw an oval for the ear. Add guidelines for the shoulders and arms.

3

Draw the outline of Monroe's neck, shoulder, and arms. Add ovals for the hands. Draw almond-shaped ovals for the eyes.

4

Erase the guidelines of the body. Erase the eye guide. Draw lines inside the eye. Add eyebrows, a nose, and lips. Draw the cheek and jaw. Create the arm of the chair using a curved line.

5

Erase the guidelines for the nose and mouth. Erase part of the head oval. Add the hair and ear lines. Draw the sleeves of Monroe's jacket.

6

Erase the rest of the guidelines. Draw lines around the eyes and add pupils. Draw the collar of his shirt and the edge of his jacket. Draw his hand, which holds a piece of paper. Draw the table.

7

Draw the jacket collar and soften the line of his shoulder. Draw the other hand. Erase the first hand's guide oval. Draw paper on the table and lines on the armchair. Add lines to his chin.

8

Erase the hand oval and the lines of his body that go through his clothing. Finish with detailed shading using the side of your pencil. His jacket and eyes are dark. Shade in the background.

Timeline

1758 James Monroe is born in Westmoreland County, Virginia, on April 28.

1774 Monroe attends the College of William and Mary.

1776–1778 Monroe joins the Third Virginia Regiment. He fights in the Revolutionary War battles of Harlem Heights, White Plains, Trenton, Brandywine, Germantown, and Monmouth.

1780 Monroe studies law under Virginian governor Thomas Jefferson.

1782 Monroe is elected to the Virginia House of Delegates.

1783 Monroe is first elected a Virginian delegate to the Congress of the Confederation. He serves for three years.

1786 Monroe marries Elizabeth Kortright.

1787 Monroe is elected to the Virginia Assembly.

1790 Monroe is elected U.S. senator.

1794 Monroe serves as U.S. minister to France.

1799 Monroe is elected governor of Virginia.

1803 Monroe and Livingston negotiate the Louisiana Purchase from France.

1811 Monroe becomes James Madison's secretary of state.

1812 The United States declares war on Britain.

1814 British forces occupy and burn Washington, D.C.
Monroe replaces John Armstrong as secretary of war.
The Treaty of Ghent is signed, which ends the War of 1812.

1816 Monroe is elected president of the United States.

1820 James Monroe wins reelection as president.

1821 The American Colonization Society founds Liberia.

1823 Monroe builds Oak Hill estate.

1831 James Monroe dies on July 4, in New York City.

Glossary

American Revolution (uh-MER-uh-ken reh-vuh-LOO-shun) Battles that soldiers from the colonies fought against Britain for freedom, from 1775 to 1783.

autobiography (ah-toh-by-AH-gruh-fee) The story of a person's life written by that person.

Board of Visitors (BORD UV VIH-zih-terz) A group that helps manage the University of Virginia.

colonization (kah-lih-nih-ZAY-shun) The settling of new land and the claiming of it for the government of another country.

compromise (KOM-pruh-myz) To give up something, to reach an agreement.

declare (dih-KLAYR) To announce officially.

defeated (dih-FEET-ed) Won against someone in a contest or battle.

delegates (DEH-li-gets) People acting for other people or groups.

diplomat (DIH-pluh-mat) A person whose job is to handle relations between his or her country and other countries.

doctrine (DOK-trin) Something that is taught or stated such as a system of beliefs.

executive (eg-ZEK-yoo-tiv) Referring to the top branch of government, which includes the president.

foreign (FOR-in) Outside one's own country.

heroism (HER-oh-wih-zem) Brave action or behavior.

militia (muh-LIH-shuh) A group of people who are trained and ready to fight when needed.

monarchy (MAH-nar-kee) A government run by a king or a queen.

negotiate (nih-GOH-shee-ayt) To talk over and arrange terms for an agreement.

neutral (NOO-trul) Not on either side of an argument or a war.

obligations (ah-bluh-GAY-shunz) Things one has to do.

plantation (plan-TAY-shun) A very large farm where crops were grown.

role model (ROHL MAH-dul) A person who shows others good behavior.

Index

Web Sites

Due to the changing nature of Internet links, PowerKids Press has developed an online list of Web sites related to the subject of this book. This site is updated regularly. Please use this link to access the list:
www.powerkidslinks.com/kgdpusa/monroe/